180 Days of Cursive
Advanced

Publishing Credits
Corinne Burton, M.A.Ed., *Publisher*
Emily R. Smith, M.A.Ed., *Senior VP of Content Development*
Véronique Bos, *Vice President of Creative*
Andrew Greene, M.A.Ed., *Senior Content Manager*
Jill Malcolm, *Graphic Designer*

Standards
© Copyright 2007–2021 Texas Education Agency (TEA). All Rights Reserved.
© 2012 English–Language Arts Content Standards for California Public Schools by the California Department of Education.
© Copyright 2010 National Governors Association Center for Best Practices and Council of Chief State School Officers. All rights reserved.

Image Credits: all images from iStock and/or Shutterstock

The classroom teacher may reproduce copies of materials in this book for classroom use only. The reproduction of any part for an entire school or school system is strictly prohibited. No part of this publication may be transmitted, stored, or recorded in any form without written permission from the publisher.

Website addresses included in this book are public domain and may be subject to changes or alterations of content after publication of this product. Shell Education does not take responsibility for the future accuracy or relevance and appropriateness of website addresses included in this book. Please contact the company if you come across any inappropriate or inaccurate website addresses, and they will be corrected in product reprints.

All companies, websites, and products mentioned in this book are registered trademarks of their respective owners or developers and are used in this book strictly for editorial purposes. No commercial claim to their use is made by the author or the publisher.

A division of Teacher Created Materials
5482 Argosy Avenue
Huntington Beach, CA 92649
www.tcmpub.com/shell-education
ISBN 978-1-0876-6244-2
© 2023 Shell Educational Publishing, Inc.

Table of Contents

Introduction
Foundations for Cursive 5
Getting Ready to Write 6
Letter Presentation Order 8
Sight Words 9
How to Use This Book 10

Weekly Practice Pages
Week 1: *Cc* 13
Week 2: *Aa* 18
Week 3: *Dd* 23
Week 4: Numbers and Review 28
Week 5: *Gg* 33
Week 6: *Ee* 38
Week 7: *Ll* 43
Week 8: Numbers and Review 48
Week 9: *Ff* 53
Week 10: *Hh* 58
Week 11: *Tt* 63
Week 12: Numbers and Review 68
Week 13: *Pp* 73
Week 14: *Uu* 78
Week 15: Numbers and Review 83
Week 16: *Yy* 88
Week 17: *Ii* 93
Week 18: Numbers and Review 98
Week 19: *Jj* 103
Week 20: *Oo* 108
Week 21: Numbers and Review 113
Week 22: *Ww* 118
Week 23: *Bb* 123

Table of Contents (cont.)

Weekly Practice Pages

Week 24: Numbers and Review	128
Week 25: *Vv*	133
Week 26: *Kk*	138
Week 27: Numbers and Review	143
Week 28: *Rr*	148
Week 29: *Ss*	153
Week 30: Numbers and Review	158
Week 31: *Nn*	163
Week 32: *Mm*	168
Week 33: Numbers and Review	173
Week 34: *Xx*	178
Week 35: *Qq*	183
Week 36: *Zz*	188

Appendix

Lowercase Letter Guide	193
Uppercase Letter Guide	194
Number Guide	195
Answer Key	196
Suggested Websites	200
Digital Resources	200

Introduction

Foundations for Cursive

Welcome to *180 Days of Cursive: Advanced*! Students will practice writing in cursive, including strokes and connections. They will not only continue to form individual letters, but also make connections between letters to write words and sentences. These practice pages provide fun and engaging ways for young learners to develop good handwriting habits.

Hand-eye Coordination

Hand-eye coordination is essential for handwriting. Students track lines with their eyes to guide, direct, and control hand movement. Coordination allows students to write on the line, properly space letters, write proper letter size, and more. This developmental approach is also seen in research-based programs, such as Handwriting Without Tears. Hand-eye coordination is reinforced throughout this book through engaging, age-appropriate activities and practice pages.

Drawing

Drawing helps students develop fine-motor skills that extend to handwriting, such as holding a writing instrument correctly and applying the correct amount of force and speed to mark paper. Just as with print, students benefit from drawing as a way to build motor control in a fun and engaging manner. Drawing keeps writers engaged through fun activities and practice pages.

Tracing

Tracing reinforces basic stroke formation along with hand-eye coordination. As a fine-tuning skill, tracing helps students develop fine-motor skills as they continue to improve their cursive. Students also become more aware of spacing, which is essential for writing well in cursive.

 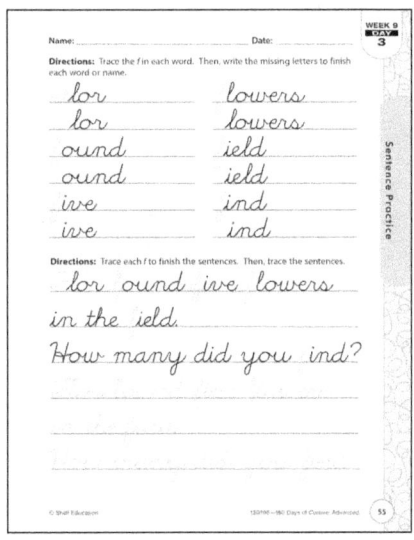 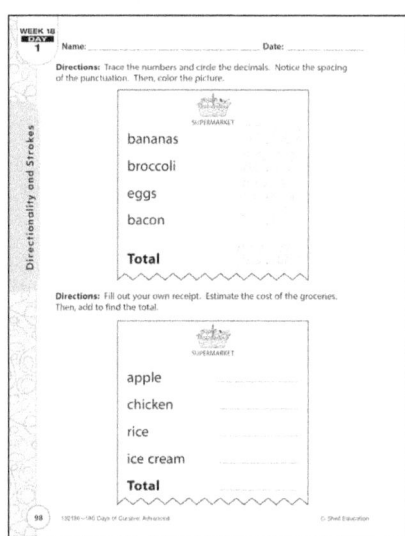

Introduction

Getting Ready to Write

Pencil Grip

Students will naturally find their dominant hand as they learn to properly grip writing instruments. Help students decide which hand is more comfortable to write with, and guide them to alternate hands if they show no clear preference. Teach students a pencil grip with their pointer finger on the top, thumb on the side, and three fingers below the pencil to support the grip. Encourage students to use this pencil grip as they work through the pages of the book.

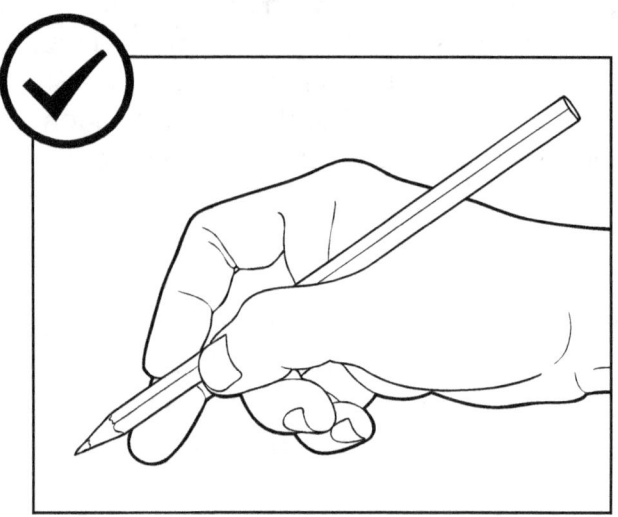
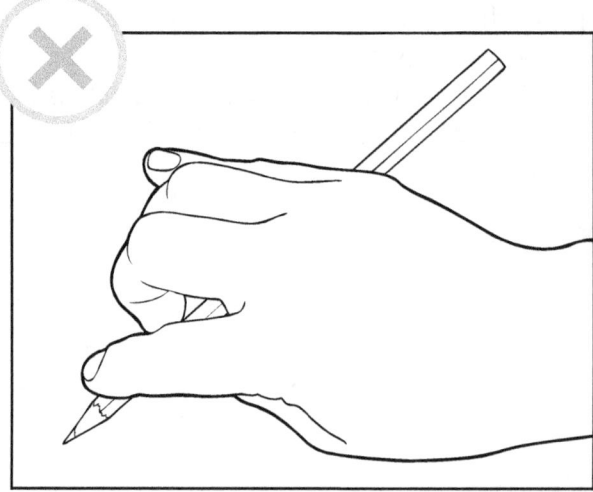

Pencil Weight (Writing Too Hard or Too Soft)

Students should press down on the pencil with medium weight. Demonstrate the proper pressure to use when writing—not too hard and not too soft. Bring students' attention to the color of the line when the correct weight is used.

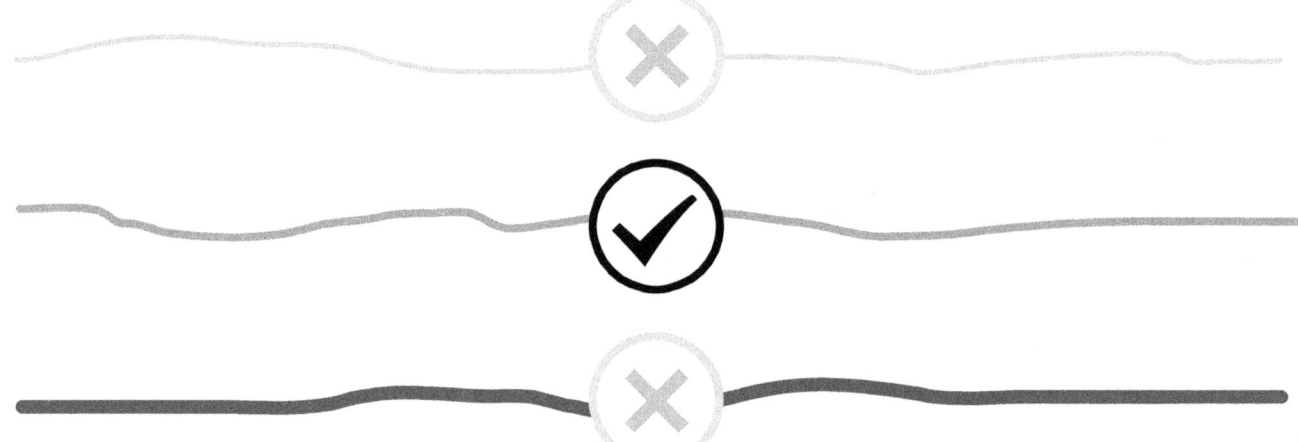

Introduction

Letter Spacing

Teach students proper letter spacing within a word and between words in a sentence. While cursive letters within a word connect, each letter should be defined and each connecting stroke should form a cohesive transition. As students grasp spacing within words, demonstrate the required spacing between sentences. Remind students that there should be no connecting strokes between words, and that there should be a space just like when printing. Reinforce letter spacing as students practice writing sentences in the review pages.

Letter Angle

Cursive should be written at a slight angle. Demonstrate writing at a slope for students to observe and encourage them to match the angle of the letters. Show students how to hold the page at an angle with their nondominant hand to help create the proper letter shapes. Encourage students to try different ways of holding the page to find the most comfortable position for writing—left-handed and right-handed students may benefit from holding the book at different angles as they write.

Introduction

Letter Presentation Order

To give students a strong foundation in handwriting, this book builds off the smallest handwriting units—strokes. By presenting letters by strokes used for cursive letters instead of alphabetical order, students can more easily make connections on how to write them. The letter presentation order also takes into account whether the letter is formed with a stroke from the top or bottom. Presenting letters by stroke also gives students ample practice time to create and refine motor control when creating letter strokes. The use of repetition in presenting strokes across multiple weeks provides the practice young learners need to increase proficiency.

Introduction

Sight Words

This program takes a holistic approach to handwriting, teaching not only individual letters but also how they fit into words and sentences. High-frequency words pulled from Dr. Edward Fry's Instant Words list and Dr. Edward Dolch's Most Common Words list allow students to practice words they will see and write frequently. The use of these sight words to practice handwriting increases letter awareness as students are exposed to these letters and words in other age-appropriate learning materials.

Name: _____ **Date:** _____

WEEK 1 DAY 3

Directions: Trace the *c* in each word. Then, write the missing letters to finish each word or name.

harlie   abinet
harlie   abinet
an   heck
an   heck
at   limb
at   limb

Directions: Trace each *c* to finish the sentences. Then, trace the sentences.

harlie the   at an limb on the abinet.
an you heck if harlie is on the abinet?

Charlie the cat can climb on the cabinet.
Can you check if Charlie is on the cabinet?

Sentence Practice

© Shell Education   130196—180 Days of Cursive: Advanced   15

Introduction

How to Use This Book

Day 1

Directionality and Strokes

180 Days of Cursive: Advanced prioritizes giving students a strong foundation as they begin practicing. Before each letter is introduced, students have a chance to practice strokes—the basic shapes that make up letters. Students practice the individual strokes of the lowercase and uppercase letter before applying all the strokes to write.

Day 2

Cursive Uppercase and Lowercase

Uppercase and lowercase letters are introduced after the relevant letter strokes are introduced and practiced, setting students up for success. Students benefit from tracing letters, writing letters independently, and writing letters as parts of words. Students use their understanding of letter shapes, spacing, and connection. They are also applying their skills to vocabulary and sight words.

Introduction

Day 3 — Sentence Practice

Students practice words and sentences with each sample letter. By using the letters in sentences, students demonstrate spatial awareness and practice proper punctuation. Students go over each letter presented through alliterative sentences and writing prompts. Repetition of high-frequency words in sentences also reinforces cursive writing retention.

Day 4 — Activity

Activities give students opportunities to practice strokes, directionality, and letter recognition in engaging ways. At the fourth, fifth, and sixth grade levels, it is important to focus on refining fine-motor skills and making practice fun.

Day 5 — Activity or Review

A key to mastering cursive is repetition. Students are presented with activities on letter weeks and reviews on number weeks to give them opportunities to practice. The activities and reviews build on material presented to practice connections and move toward more independent writing. The reviews also provide opportunities to improve cursive writing through repetition.

Introduction

Standards Correlations

Shell Education is committed to producing educational materials that are research and standards based. To support this effort, this resource is correlated to the academic standards of all 50 states, the District of Columbia, the Department of Defense Dependent Schools, and the Canadian provinces. A correlation is also provided for key professional educational organizations.

To print a customized correlation report for your state, please visit our website at **www.tcmpub.com/administrators/correlations** and follow the online directions. If you require assistance in printing correlation reports, please contact the Customer Service Department at 1-800-858-7339.

Stroke and Directionality (Day 1)	**Foundational Skills: Adjust grasp and body position for increased control in drawing and writing.** • Demonstrate proper finger grasp. • Begin using nondominant hand to hold paper to maintain control.
Cursive Uppercase and Lowercase (Day 2)	**Foundational Skills: Print all upper- and lowercase letters.** • Recognize and print all upper- and lowercase letters of the alphabet. **Foundational Skills: Capitalize dates and names of people.** • Demonstrate understanding of capitalization. **Foundational Skills: Capitalize holidays, product names, and geographic names.** • Demonstrate understanding of capitalization.
Sentence Practice (Day 3)	**Foundational Skills: Use end punctuation for sentences.** • Demonstrate understanding of the organization and basic features of print.
Activity (Day 4)	**Foundational Skills: Practice words phonetically, drawing on phonemic awareness and spelling conventions.** • Demonstrate the ability to decode new vocabulary through phonemic and spelling awareness.
Review (Day 5)	**Foundational Skills: Use frequently occurring nouns and verbs.** • Begin reading and writing high-frequency nouns and verbs. • Demonstrate basic comprehension of nouns and verbs through sight words.

Name: _____ Date: _____

WEEK 1 DAY 1

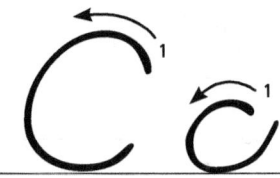

Directions: Trace each curve. Then, copy each row.

Directions: Trace each C. Practice connecting each C without lifting your pencil. Then, copy each row.

Directionality and Strokes

WEEK 1 DAY 2

Name: _____ Date: _____

Directions: Trace each letter. Then, practice writing your own letters.

Directions: Trace each letter. Then, copy the patterns.

Cursive Uppercase & Lowercase

Name: _____ Date: _____

WEEK 1 DAY 3

Directions: Trace the *c* in each word. Then, write each missing letter to finish each word or name.

Charlie   cabinet
Charlie   cabinet
can   check
can   check
cat   climb
cat   climb

Directions: Trace each *c* to finish the sentences. Then, trace the sentences.

Charlie the cat can climb on the cabinet. Can you check if Charlie is on the cabinet?

Charlie the cat can climb on the cabinet. Can you check if Charlie is on the cabinet?

Sentence Practice

WEEK 1 DAY 4

Name: _____ Date: _____

Directions: Complete the word search.

```
l t e o n f e y o c t j f n f
m p e a c p s z l q j s m a o
z n e a a g r m c c d g h o e
k c i r q k u g o n u o s w r
o c l a s s o c r e m a c e b
u v e f t m c p r z r o g p v
k s p n q n u v e v m r b a z
z e l p r s o g c p m w s i j
y n w g r r q c t s o v g y p
p a v z x u a e p r c e d f u
n o p y i l y x h m c o k x h
a u w c t b a y f l z q b h v
y w k o q v l t t v c a u z e
j l n s p o h o g r g q u g x
y n f y m a u y g m p m o x d
```

Word Bank

correct   quickly   became   contain

course   ocean   class

Name: _____ **Date:** _____

WEEK 1 DAY 5

Directions: Unscramble the letters. Then, write the words in cursive.

Clue: *vegetables*

zcucihni

ɜu hini

bercumuc

leryce

rarotc

ttuecel

ccolirob

Review

Directions: Draw your favorite foods and practice writing their names in cursive.

_____

_____

_____

_____

WEEK 2 DAY 1

Name: _____ Date: _____

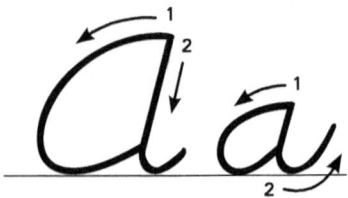

Directions: Trace each curved line and letter. Then, copy each row.

Directionality and Strokes

Name: _____ Date: _____

WEEK 2
DAY 2

Directions: Trace each letter. Then, practice writing your own letters.

Directions: Trace each letter. Then, copy the patterns.

Cursive Uppercase & Lowercase

© Shell Education   130196—180 Days of Cursive: Advanced

WEEK 2 DAY 3

Name: _____ **Date:** _____

Directions: Trace the *a* in each word. Then, write each missing letter to finish each word or name.

- aza
- aza
- always
- always
- apple
- apple

- at
- at
- ate
- ate
- an
- an

Directions: Trace each *a* to finish the sentences. Then, trace the sentences.

Aza ate an apple at a restaurant. She always eats healthy food.

Aza ate an apple at a restaurant. She always eats healthy food.

Name: _____ Date: _____

Directions: Fill in the missing letters to answer the riddles.

I look like a monkey, but I don't have a tail.

I'm __a__ __a__pe!

I'm big and green and like to swim. People get scared because of my toothy grin.

I'm __a__n __a__lligator.

I have a hard gray shell and like to eat plants. Sometimes, I might also eat some ants!

I'm __a__n __a__rmadillo.

WEEK 2 DAY 5

Name: _____ **Date:** _____

Directions: Unscramble the letters. Then, write the words in cursive.

Clue: animals

lalirotag lligtor _____ *epa* _____

guraaj _____ *dilloamar* _____

amelc _____ *heetahc* _____

Directions: Draw your favorite animal and practice writing its name in cursive.

Name: _____

22 130196—180 Days of Cursive: Advanced © Shell Education

Name: _____ Date: _____

WEEK 3
DAY 1

Directions: Trace each curved line and letter. Then, copy each row.

Directionality and Strokes

WEEK 3 DAY 2

Name: _____ Date: _____

Directions: Trace each letter. Then, practice writing your own letters.

Directions: Trace each letter. Then, copy the patterns.

Name: _____ Date: _____

Directions: Trace the *d* in each word. Then, write each missing letter to finish each word or name.

Dave

ave

o

o

decide

ecide

did

id

dance

ance

didn't

idn't

Directions: Trace each *d* to finish the sentences. Then, trace the sentences.

Did Dave decide to do the dance?
No, he didn't.

Did Dave decide to do the dance?
No, he didn't.

WEEK 3 DAY 4

Name: _____ Date: _____

Directions: Solve each puzzle. What are the words and pictures saying?

Activity

T
O
W
N

owntown

D movie
D movie
D movie

_3___ movie_

L
O
A
D

ownlo

EYE
EYE

_eye sh___ow_

Name: _____ Date: _____

WEEK 3 DAY 5

Review

Directions: Fill in the missing letters to answer the riddles.

What's hot and dry and full of sand?

a ___esert___

Where does Thursday come after Friday?

the ___i tionary___

What can you catch but not throw?

a ___ol___

WEEK 4 DAY 1

Name: _____ Date: _____

Directions: Trace the numbers. Fill out the rest of the numbers on the clock. Then, write the time shown on the clock.

Time: _____

Name: _____ Date: _____

Directions: Trace each number. Then, practice writing your own numbers.

0 _____

1 _____

2 _____

3 _____

4 _____

5 _____

6 _____

7 _____

8 _____

9 _____

WEEK 4 DAY 3

Name: _____ Date: _____

Directions: Count each set of items. Trace the words in the sentences, and write the number on each line. Then, choose one of the sentences to write on your own.

Sentence Practice

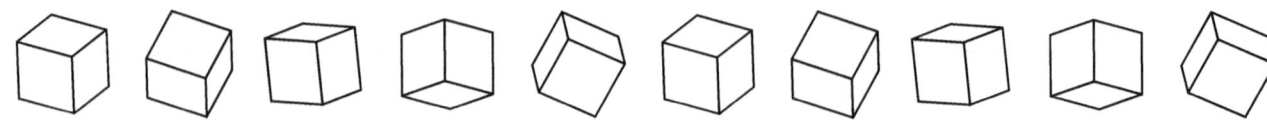

There are _____ cubes.
_____

There are _____ apples.
_____

There is _____ bike.
_____

I have _____ cents.
_____

Sentence: _____

Name: _____ Date: _____

Directions: Use complete sentences to answer the questions in your best cursive.

How old are you?

_____

_____

How long is your hair? Estimate how many inches.

_____

_____

How many siblings do you have?

_____

_____

How many hats are you wearing?

_____

_____

How many pieces of chocolate did you eat today?

_____

_____

WEEK 4 DAY 5

Name: _____ Date: _____

Directions: Trace each letter. Write your own letters to fill each line. Then, trace the sentence, and write it on your own.

Review

c _____

_____

C _____

_____

a _____

_____

a _____

_____

d _____

_____

D _____

_____

Dani likes to eat cake. _____

_____

32 130196—180 Days of Cursive: Advanced © Shell Education

Name: _____ Date: _____

WEEK 5 DAY 1

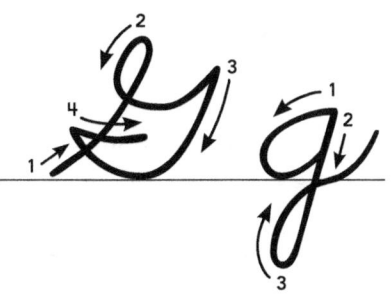

Directions: Trace each curved line and letter. Then, copy each row.

Directionality and Strokes

Name: _____ **Date:** _____

Directions: Trace each letter. Then, practice writing your own letters.

Directions: Trace each letter. Then, copy the patterns.

Name: _____ Date: _____

WEEK 5 DAY 3

Directions: Trace the *g* in each word. Then, write each missing letter to finish each word or name.

Gio   green
io   reen
grapes go
rapes   o
got   going
ot   oing

Directions: Trace each *g* to finish the sentences. Then, trace the sentences.

Gio got green grapes for the party.
Are you going to go?

Gio got green grapes for the party.
Are you going to go?

Sentence Practice

© Shell Education   130196—180 Days of Cursive: Advanced   35

WEEK 5 DAY 4

Name: _____ **Date:** _____

Directions: Solve each puzzle. What are the words and pictures saying?

VEG

_ve_ _etables_

Get it
Get it
Get it
Get it

for _et_ _it_

noon good

___oo___
fternoon

Way go go

way _to_ ___o___

Name: _____ **Date:** _____

WEEK 5 DAY 5

Directions: Unscramble the letters. Write the words in cursive. Draw a picture using your favorite color. Then, write a sentence describing your picture.

Clue: *colors*

energ _____   yarg _____

green

onager _____   eigeb _____

ghtrib yllowe _____   agatnem _____

_____

_____

Review

WEEK 6 DAY 1

Name: _____ Date: _____

Directions: Trace each loop and letter. Then, copy each row.

Name: _____ Date: _____

WEEK 6 DAY 2

Directions: Trace each letter. Then, practice writing your own letters.

ℓ ℓ ℓ ℓ ℓ ℓ ℓ ℓ ℓ ℓ ℓ ℓ

ℓ

ℓ

E E E E E E E E E E

E

E

Directions: Trace each letter. Then, copy the patterns.

Eℓ Eℓ Eℓ Eℓ Eℓ Eℓ Eℓ

Eℓℓ Eℓℓ Eℓℓ Eℓℓ Eℓℓ E

ℓℓℓ E ℓℓℓ E ℓℓℓ E ℓℓℓ E ℓℓℓ

Cursive Uppercase & Lowercase

© Shell Education 130196—180 Days of Cursive: Advanced

WEEK 6 DAY 3

Name: _____ Date: _____

Directions: Trace the *e* in each word. Then, write each missing letter to finish each word or name.

Emi_l   _ggs
Emi_l   _ggs
v_ry   _v_n
v_ry   _v_n
_ats   _ight
_ats   _ight

Directions: Trace each *e* to finish the sentences. Then, trace the sentences.

Emi_l _ats _ight _ggs
v_ry day.
I don't _v_n lik_ _ggs!

Emiel eats eight eggs
every day.
I don't even like eggs!

40 130196—180 Days of Cursive: Advanced   © Shell Education

Name: _____ Date: _____

Directions: Solve each puzzle. What are the words and pictures saying?

LEM / ADE	FAST
l mon	*br kf st*
T 🛍️	HEAD HEAD HEAD HEAD
t b	*for h d*

WEEK 6 DAY 5

Name: _____ Date: _____

Directions: Fill in the missing letters to answer the riddles. Then, write a riddle in your best cursive to share with someone.

You see it once in June, three times in September, and never in May. What is it?

th_ l_tt_r

I am an odd number. Take away a letter and I become even. What number am I?

s_v_n

What goes up but never comes down?

a__

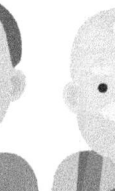

_____

_____

_____

Review

Name: _____ Date: _____

WEEK 7 DAY 1

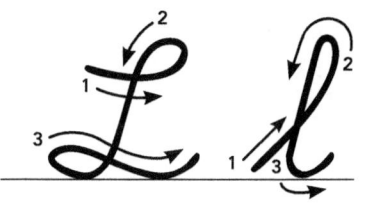

Directions: Trace each loop and letter. Then, copy each row.

Directionality and Strokes

WEEK 7 DAY 2

Name: _____ Date: _____

Cursive Uppercase & Lowercase

Directions: Trace each letter. Then, practice writing your own letters.

ℓ ℓ ℓ ℓ ℓ ℓ ℓ ℓ ℓ ℓ ℓ ℓ ℓ ℓ ℓ

ℓ

ℓ

L L L L L L L L L

L

L

Directions: Trace each letter. Then, copy the patterns.

Lℓ Lℓ Lℓ Lℓ Lℓ Lℓ Lℓ

ℓL ℓL ℓL ℓL ℓL ℓL ℓL

Lℓℓ Lℓℓ Lℓℓ Lℓℓ Lℓℓ Lℓℓ

44 130196—180 Days of Cursive: Advanced © Shell Education

Name: _____ **Date:** _____

Directions: Trace each *l*. Then, write each missing letter to finish each word or name.

Levi   *late*
evi   *ate*
Leah   *a*
eah   *a*
library   *let*
ibrary   *et*

Directions: Trace each *l* to finish the sentences. Then, trace the sentences.

Leah, let Levi return your books to the library. They're all late.

Leah, let Levi return your books to the library. They're all late.

WEEK 7 DAY 4

Name: _____ Date: _____

Directions: Unscramble the letters. Then, write the words in cursive.

Clue: activities

licmb a oumntina
limb mount in
_____

og hnga dingilg
_____

earnl ot veidr
_____

stenil ot cisum
_____

andl an rpanelia
_____

fyl a itek
_____

Name: _____ Date: _____

Directions: Fill in the missing letters to answer the riddles.

What gets wetter the more it dries?

___ *tow* ___

What can fill a room but doesn't take up space?

i ___ *ht*

What do you fill with empty hands?

___ *ov* ___ *s*

Directions: Trace the sentences. Then, practice writing them on your own.

Lovely lace covered her face.

_____

_____

Lolo sings lullabies.

_____

WEEK 8 DAY 1

Name: _____ Date: _____

Directions: Color the numbers. Then, color the remainder of the picture. Write a complete sentence to tell how much money is on the page.

_____

_____

_____

Name: _____ Date: _____

WEEK 8 DAY 2

Directions: Trace each amount. Then, practice writing the dollar amounts. Remember to use the dollar sign.

$10.00 _____

$20.00 _____

$30.00 _____

$40.00 _____

$50.00 _____

$60.00 _____

$70.00 _____

$80.00 _____

$90.00 _____

$100.00 _____

Numbers

WEEK 8 DAY 3

Name: _____ Date: _____

Sentence Practice

Directions: Count each set of items. Trace the words in the sentences, and write the number on each line. Then, choose one of the sentences to write on your own.

There are _____ cubes.
_____

There are _____ apples.
_____

There are _____ wheels.
_____

I have _____ cents.
_____

Sentence: _____

50 130196—180 Days of Cursive: Advanced

Name: _____ Date: _____

Directions: Use complete sentences to answer the questions in your best cursive.

How many toes do you have?

_____

_____

How many shows do you like?

_____

_____

How many points did you get in the last game you played?

_____

_____

How old will you be when you finish school?

_____

_____

How tall are you? Estimate your height in inches.

_____

_____

WEEK 8 DAY 5

Name: _____ Date: _____

Directions: Trace each letter. Write your own letters to fill each line. Then, trace the sentence, and write it on your own.

Review

J _____

_____

g _____

_____

e _____

_____

E _____

_____

l _____

_____

L _____

_____

Gino used gel in his hair.

_____

Name: _____ Date: _____

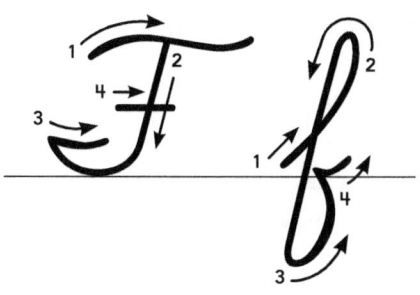

Directions: Trace each loop and curved line. Then, copy each row.

Directionality and Strokes

WEEK 9 DAY 2

Name: _____ **Date:** _____

Directions: Trace each letter. Then, practice writing your own letters.

Directions: Trace each letter. Then, copy the patterns.

WEEK 9 DAY 3

Name: _____ Date: _____

Directions: Trace the *f* in each word. Then, write each missing letter to finish each word or name.

Flor   flowers
_lor   _lowers
found   field
_ound   _ield
five   find
_ive   _ind

Directions: Trace each *f* to finish the sentences. Then, trace the sentences.

Flor found five flowers in the field. How many did you find?

Flor found five flowers in the field. How many did you find?

Sentence Practice

WEEK 9 DAY 4

Name: _____ Date: _____

Directions: Solve each puzzle. What are the words and pictures saying?

TTTT years / years	fi4lm
forty years	_or ign_ / _ilm_

Water (curved downward)	come table / table / table / table
_w t rf ll_	_comfort bl_

Name: _____ Date: _____

WEEK 9 DAY 5

Directions: Unscramble the letters. Then, write the words in cursive.

Clue: *feelings*

hankfult

thankful

fercei

_____

oyulfj

_____

opfuleh

_____

ustratedrf

_____

lueredtsf

_____

Review

WEEK 10 DAY 1

Name: _____ Date: _____

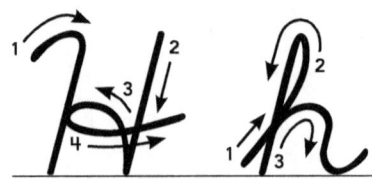

Directions: Trace each curved line and letter. Then, copy each row.

Directionality and Strokes

Name: _____ **Date:** _____

Directions: Trace each letter. Then, practice writing your own letters.

Directions: Trace each letter. Then, copy the patterns.

WEEK 10 DAY 3

Name: _____ Date: _____

Directions: Trace the *h* in each word. Then, write each missing letter to finish each word or name.

Hank   *hundreds*
___ank   ___undreds
Hichul   *horses*
___ichul   ___orses
has   *how*
___as   ___ow

Directions: Trace each *h* to finish the sentences. Then, trace the sentences.

Hank has hundreds of horses.

How many does Hichul have?

Name: _____ Date: _____

WEEK 10 DAY 4

Directions: Solve each puzzle. What are the words and pictures saying?

T
O
U
C
H

tou down

i w y

on yb

nafish
nafish

tun ish

WEEK 10 DAY 5

Name: _____ Date: _____

Directions: Fill in the missing letters to solve the riddles.

A barrel of water weighs 20 pounds. What must you add to it to make it weigh 12 pounds?

___ _ol_ ___

Why don't lobsters share?

_t_ ___ _y'r_ ___ _s_ ___ _llfis_ ___

What kind of room has no windows or doors?

___ _mus_ _room_

Directions: Trace the sentences. Then, practice writing them on your own.

Happy heroes help others.

How do you hold the handle?

Name: _____   **Date:** _____

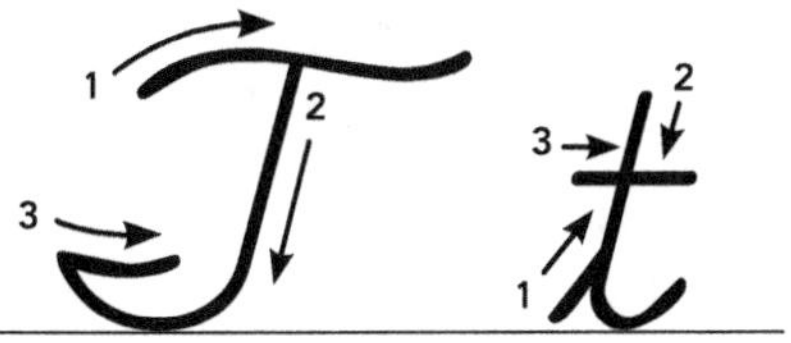

WEEK 11 DAY 1

Directions: Trace each curved line and letter. Then, copy each row.

Directionality and Strokes

WEEK 11 DAY 2

Name: _____ Date: _____

Directions: Trace each letter. Then, practice writing your own letters.

Directions: Trace each letter. Then, copy the patterns.

Name: _____ **Date:** _____

WEEK 11 DAY 3

Directions: Trace the *t* in each word. Then, write each missing letter to finish each word or name.

Thalia   tea
Thalia   tea
thinks   takes
thinks   takes
tastiest   the
tastiest   the

Directions: Trace each *t* to finish the sentences. Then, trace the sentences.

Thalia thinks the tastiest tea is jasmine. It takes patience to brew.

Thalia thinks the tastiest tea is jasmine. It takes patience to brew.

WEEK 11 DAY 4

Name: _____ Date: _____

Directions: Fill in the missing letters to solve each riddle. Then, write a riddle for a friend to solve.

What can clap without hands?

___*und*___*r*___

What begins with *T*, ends with *T*, and has *T* in it?

___*pot*___

What is easier to get into than out of?

___*rouble*___

_____

_____

_____

Name: _____ Date: _____

WEEK 11 DAY 5

Directions: Unscramble the letters. Then, write the words in cursive.

Clue: plants

almp eert   oletiv
palm tree

ulipt   ctusca

tnim   aterw llyi

Review

WEEK 12 DAY 1

Name: _____ Date: _____

Directions: Trace the numbers. Write the title of your favorite movie with show times. Then, color the picture.

Directionality and Strokes

The Action Movie
3:45 5:30 6:10

Laugh Your Socks Off
11:50 2:25 4:15

Animated Wonderland
10:30 12:15 3:35

WEEK 12 DAY 2

Name: _____ Date: _____

Directions: Trace each number. Then, practice writing your own numbers.

1:00 _____

2:00 _____

3:00 _____

4:00 _____

5:00 _____

6:00 _____

7:00 _____

8:00 _____

9:00 _____

10:00 _____

11:00 _____

12:00 _____

Numbers

WEEK 12 DAY 3

Name: _____ Date: _____

Directions: Count each set of items. Trace the words in the sentences, and write the number on each line. Then, choose one of the sentences to write on your own.

Sentence Practice

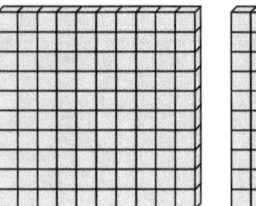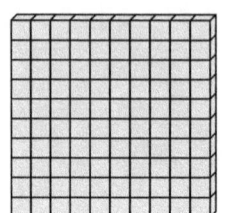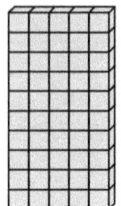

There are _____ cubes.
_____

There are _____ apples.
_____

There are _____ wheels.
_____

I have _____ cents.
_____

_____

Name: _____ Date: _____

Directions: Complete the number line.

WEEK 12 DAY 4

0, 50, 100, ____, ____, 250, ____, ____, ____, ____, ____, ____, ____, 700, ____, ____, ____, ____, ____

WEEK 12 DAY 5

Name: _____ Date: _____

Directions: Trace each letter. Write your own letters to fill each line. Then, trace the sentence, and write it on your own.

f

F

h

H

t

T

Fresh tomatoes are on sale!

Name: _____ Date: _____

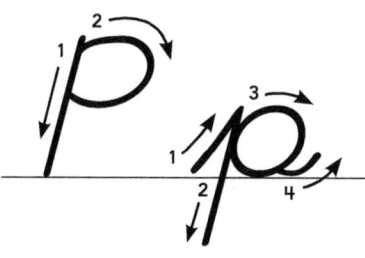

Directions: Trace each line and letter. Then, copy each row.

WEEK 13 DAY 2

Name: _____ Date: _____

Directions: Trace each letter. Then, practice writing your own letters.

p p p p p p p p p p p p

p

p

P P P P P P P P P P P P

P

P

Directions: Trace each letter. Then, copy the patterns.

Pp Pp Pp Pp Pp Pp Pp Pp

Ppp Ppp Ppp Ppp

ppP ppP ppP ppP

Cursive Uppercase & Lowercase

Name: _____ Date: _____

Directions: Copy the words. Then, fill the lines.

place _____

pet _____

cheap _____

Directions: Use the words above to finish the sentences.

What is your favorite _____ ?

I like the farm because I can _____ animals.

It is very _____ to visit the farm. It does not cost any money!

WEEK 13 DAY 4

Name: _____ Date: _____

Directions: Solve each puzzle. What are the words and pictures saying?

APPLE π

_____ i

↑ uu

u to you

e
k
a
w

w k u

POT 8 o

ot to

Name: _____ **Date:** _____

WEEK 13 DAY 5

Directions: Unscramble the letters. Then, write the words in cursive.

Clue: *fruits*

pplea — *apple*

ayappa

pricota

eprag

neappleip

mulp

Directions: Trace the sentences. Then, practice writing them on your own.

Peter Piper picked a pepper.

How many peppers did he pick?

Review

WEEK 14 DAY 1

Name: _____ Date: _____

Directions: Trace each curved line and letter. Then, copy each row.

Name: _____ Date: _____

Directions: Trace each letter. Then, practice writing your own letters.

Directions: Trace each letter. Then, copy the patterns.

WEEK 14 DAY 2

Cursive Uppercase & Lowercase

WEEK 14 DAY 3

Name: _____ Date: _____

Directions: Copy the words. Then, fill the lines.

cut _____

up _____

cute _____

Directions: Use the words above to finish the sentences. Then, write your own sentences using the words.

The teacher hung _____ my artwork.

She thought it was very _____ !

I _____ magazine pictures to make it.

_____

_____

_____

_____

_____

Name: _____ Date: _____

WEEK 14 DAY 4

Directions: Solve each puzzle. What are the words and pictures saying?

| Try | stand / 2 |

try _o_ _on_ _u on_
_un rs nd_ _ im_

| Stood / Miss |

misun rstood

| Water / Swim |

swim und w r

Activity

© Shell Education   130196—180 Days of Cursive: Advanced   81

WEEK 14 DAY 5

Name: _____ **Date:** _____

Directions: Find rhyming words that match each definition.

lengthy tune _*long song*_____

numerals sleep _*number*_____

male pastry cook _*pie*_____

margarine knife _*butter*_____

humorous rabbit _*funny*_____

home for mice _____

Review

Name: _____ Date: _____

Directions: Trace the numbers. Then, using your best cursive, write a comment under the caption.

Dogs are the best!

10,307
526

_____

_____

_____

WEEK 15 DAY 2

Name: _____ Date: _____

Directions: Trace each number. Then, practice writing your own numbers.

1,000
_____

2,000
_____

3,000
_____

4,000
_____

5,000
_____

6,000
_____

7,000
_____

8,000
_____

9,000
_____

10,000
_____

Directions: Trace the number sentences and solve each one.

9,000 + 4,000 =
_____

8,000 − 3,000 =
_____

6,000 + 1,000 =
_____

Numbers

Name: _____ Date: _____

WEEK 15
DAY 3

Directions: Count each set of items. Trace the words in the sentences, and write the number on each line. Then, choose two of the sentences to write on your own.

There are _____ cubes.

There are _____ apples.

There are _____ wheels.

I have _____ dollars.

_____

_____

Sentence Practice

85

WEEK 15 DAY 4

Name: _____ **Date:** _____

Directions: Complete the puzzles. Include numbers 1–4 in each line and each square. Do not repeat numbers in the lines, columns, or squares.

Activity

Puzzle 1:
	3	4	
4			2
1			3
	2	1	

Puzzle 2:
			3
3	2	4	
	4	3	2
2			

Puzzle 3:
3	4	1	
	2		
		2	
	1	4	3

Name: _____ **Date:** _____

WEEK 15 DAY 5

Directions: Trace each letter. Write your own letters to fill each line. Then, trace the sentence, and write it on your own.

t

T

p

P

u

U

This umbrella is pretty.

Review

WEEK 16
DAY 1

Name: _____ Date: _____

Directions: Trace each curved line and letter. Then, copy each row.

WEEK 16 DAY 2

Name: _____ Date: _____

Directions: Trace each letter. Then, practice writing your own letters

y y y y y y y y y y y

y

y

Y Y Y Y Y Y Y Y

Y

Y

Directions: Trace each letter. Then, copy the patterns.

Yy Yy Yy Yy Yy Yy

Yyy Yyy Yyy Yyy Yyy

Cursive Uppercase & Lowercase

© Shell Education 130196—180 Days of Cursive: Advanced 89

WEEK 16 DAY 3

Name: _____ Date: _____

Directions: Copy the words. Then, fill the lines.

clay

ugly

yelled

Directions: Use the words above to finish the sentences.

My mom _____ because someone broke her cup.

It was very _____ .

My mom only liked it because my sister made it from _____ .

Name: _____ **Date:** _____

Directions: Solve each puzzle. What are the words and pictures saying?

thanks thanks
thanks thanks
thanks thanks
thanks thanks
thanks thanks

m n
nks

ook m in
_____ _____

Way go go

w o o

history
history
history

is or
r   s
is

WEEK 16 DAY 5

Name: _____ Date: _____

Directions: Unscramble the letters. Then, write the words in cursive.

Clue: adverbs

ppilyha
happily

dlyas
sadly

ngylira
angrily

ysteioulysrm
mysteriously

utiflyulaeb
beautifully

arylluefc
carefully

Review

Name: _____ Date: _____

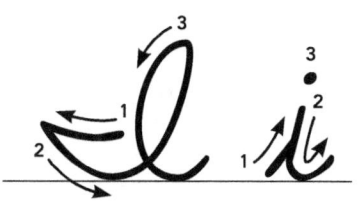

Directions: Trace each curved line and letter. Then, copy each row.

WEEK 17
DAY 1

Directionality and Strokes

93

WEEK 17 DAY 2

Name: _____ Date: _____

Directions: Trace each letter. Then, practice writing your own letters.

Cursive Uppercase & Lowercase

Directions: Trace each letter. Then, copy the patterns.

Name: _____ Date: _____

WEEK 17 DAY 3

Directions: Copy the words. Then, fill the lines.

city _____

light _____

idea _____

Directions: Use the words above to finish the sentences. Then, write your own sentences using the words.

I have an _____ .

I want to leave the _____ to see the stars.

Do you think we will be able to see stars without the _____ from the city?

_____

_____

_____

_____

_____

Sentence Practice

WEEK 17 DAY 4

Name: _____ Date: _____

Directions: Solve each puzzle. What are the words and pictures saying?

lang4uage

_or_ _n_
_n u_

abcdefghijklm nopqrstvwxyz

_m ss n_
_o_

```
    g
    n
 f  i
 i  h
 s
```

_s_
ook

MILL1ON

_on in_
mi ion

Name: _____ Date: _____

Directions: Find rhyming words that match each definition.

seafood platter — *fish* _____

excellent spruce tree — *fine* _____

fat branch — *thick* _____

bunny custom — *rabbit* _____

a hog's fake hair _____

WEEK 18 DAY 1

Name: _____ Date: _____

Directions: Trace the numbers and circle the decimals. Notice the spacing of the punctuation. Then, color the picture.

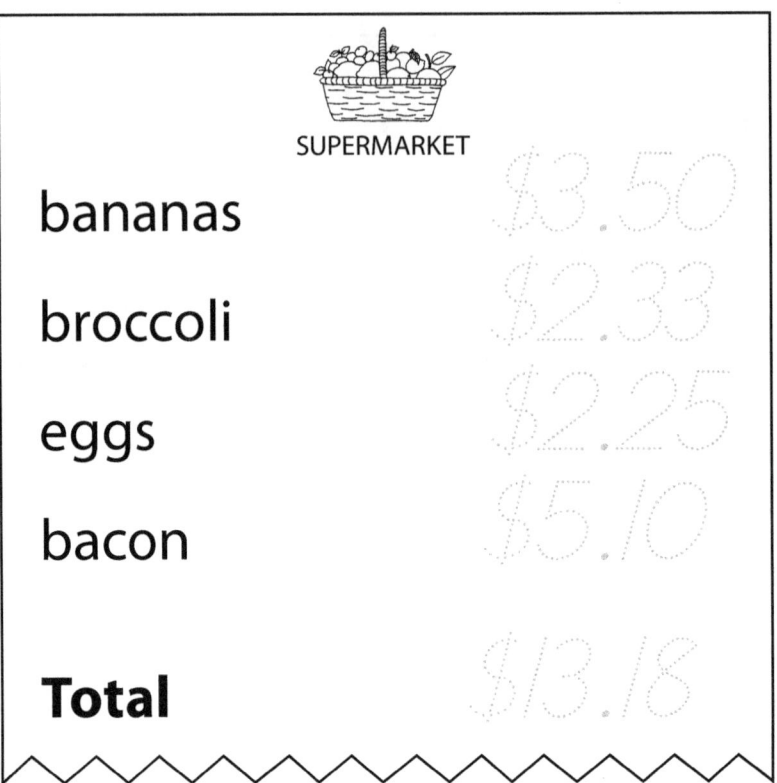

bananas $3.50

broccoli $2.33

eggs $2.25

bacon $5.10

Total $13.18

Directions: Fill out your own receipt. Estimate the cost of the groceries. Then, add to find the total.

SUPERMARKET

apple   _____

chicken   _____

rice   _____

ice cream   _____

Total   _____

Directionality and Strokes

98 130196—180 Days of Cursive: Advanced © Shell Education

Name: _____ **Date:** _____

WEEK 18 DAY 2

Directions: Trace each time. Then, practice writing your own times.

1:10
_____

2:20
_____

3:30
_____

4:45
_____

5:00
_____

6:05
_____

7:15
_____

8:00
_____

9:35
_____

10:00
_____

11:20
_____

12:55
_____

Numbers

WEEK 18 DAY 3

Name: _____ **Date:** _____

Directions: Answer the questions so they are true for you. Then, draw the hands on the clock to match. Write another sentence about your schedule.

Sentence Practice

I wake up at _____

I go to bed at _____

I start school at _____

I eat lunch at _____

_____

Name: _____ **Date:** _____

Directions: Write times in the blanks to finish the schedule so it is right for you.

_____	wake up
_____	eat breakfast
_____	read a book
_____	go to the park
_____	eat lunch
_____	watch a movie
_____	eat dinner
_____	go to bed

WEEK 18 DAY 5

Name: _____ Date: _____

Directions: Trace each letter. Then, write your own letters to fill each line.

Review

u

U

y

Y

i

I

Name: _____ Date: _____

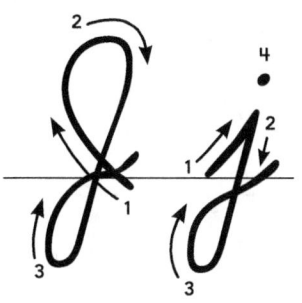

Directions: Trace each curved line and letter. Then, copy each row.

WEEK 19
DAY 1

Directionality and Strokes

WEEK 19 DAY 2

Name: _____ Date: _____

Directions: Trace each letter. Then, practice writing your own letters.

Directions: Trace each letter. Then, copy the patterns.

Name: _____ **Date:** _____

Directions: Copy the name and words. Then, fill the lines.

Judy

jelly

jug

Directions: Use the words above to finish the sentences. Then, write your own sentences using the words.

Did I tell you I bought _____ ?

I bought it from _____ .

I got a big _____ of strawberry jelly!

_____

_____

_____

_____

Name: _____ **Date:** _____

Directions: Unscramble the letters. Then, write the words in cursive.

Clue: verbs

umpj _____   goj _____
jump _____   _____

ggleju _____   ulanroj _____
_____   _____

keoj _____   glegji _____
_____   _____

Name: _____ Date: _____

Directions: Fill in the missing letters.

I'm a sweet food made from boiling sugar and fruit. What am I?

_____*lly*_____

I'm the liquid squeezed from fruits and vegetables. What am I?

_____*i*_____

I'm a precious stone that can come in many colors. What am I?

___ _____*w*_____

Directions: Trace the sentences. Then, practice writing them on your own.

Jeremiah is jumping.

Jaxson plays with Juan.

WEEK 20 DAY 1

Name: _____ Date: _____

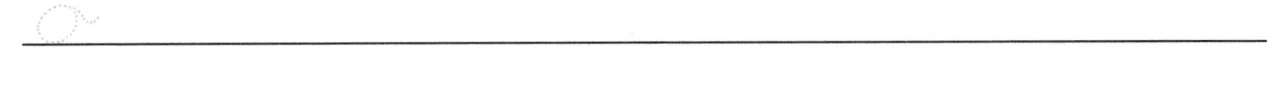

Directions: Trace each letter. Then, copy each row.

Name: _____ Date: _____

WEEK 20 DAY 2

Directions: Trace each letter. Then, practice writing your own letters.

Directions: Trace each letter. Then, copy the patterns.

Cursive Uppercase & Lowercase

© Shell Education 130196—180 Days of Cursive: Advanced 109

WEEK 20 DAY 3

Name: _____ Date: _____

Directions: Copy the words. Then, fill the lines.

dog _____

toy _____

you _____

Directions: Use the words above to finish the sentences. Then, write your own sentences using the words.

I want to tell _____ something.

I got a _____ .

I bought food, a leash, and a _____ for him.

_____

_____

_____

_____

Name: _____ **Date:** _____

Directions: Solve each puzzle. What are the words and pictures saying?

he*a*rt	↗ SECRET SECRET SECRET SECRET SECRET

broken
heart

secrets
on the rise

BAD Wolf	b k

big bad
wolf

between
a rock
and a hard place (?)

(Week 20, Day 4 — Activity)

WEEK 20 DAY 5

Name: _____ **Date:** _____

Directions: Find rhyming words that match each definition.

noisy group   _loud_ _____

toad run   _frog_ _____

paperback thief   _book_ _____

warm child   _hot_ _____

chief of police   _____

Name: _____ Date: _____

WEEK 21 DAY 1

Directions: Trace the numbers. Fill in the fourth clock with the time you go to bed.

3:10

6:45

12:00

Directionality and Strokes

**WEEK 21
DAY 2**

Name: _____ Date: _____

Directions: Trace each time. Then, practice writing your own times.

Numbers

12:30 _____

1:15 _____

2:23 _____

4:35 _____

5:01 _____

6:10 _____

7:45 _____

8:50 _____

10:59 _____

11:17 _____

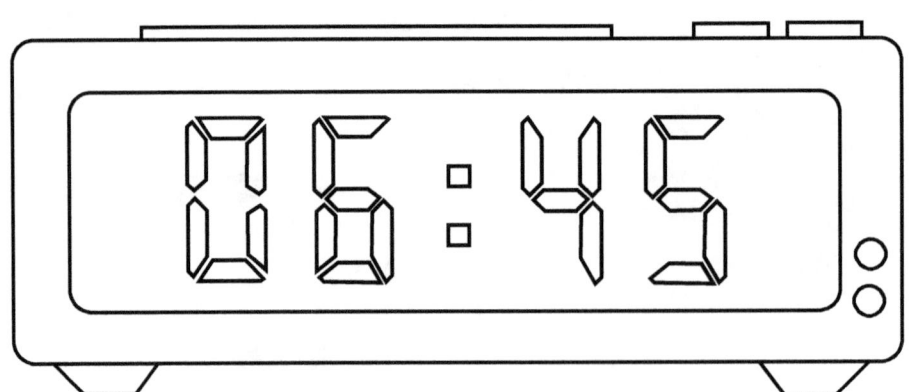

114   130196—180 Days of Cursive: Advanced   © Shell Education

Name: _____ Date: _____

Directions: Complete each sentence and write the time on each clock so the answers are right for you. Write a sentence about your day.

Right now, the time is _____ .

At _____ last night, I ate dinner.

Yesterday at _____ , I finished school.

It was _____ when I woke up this morning.

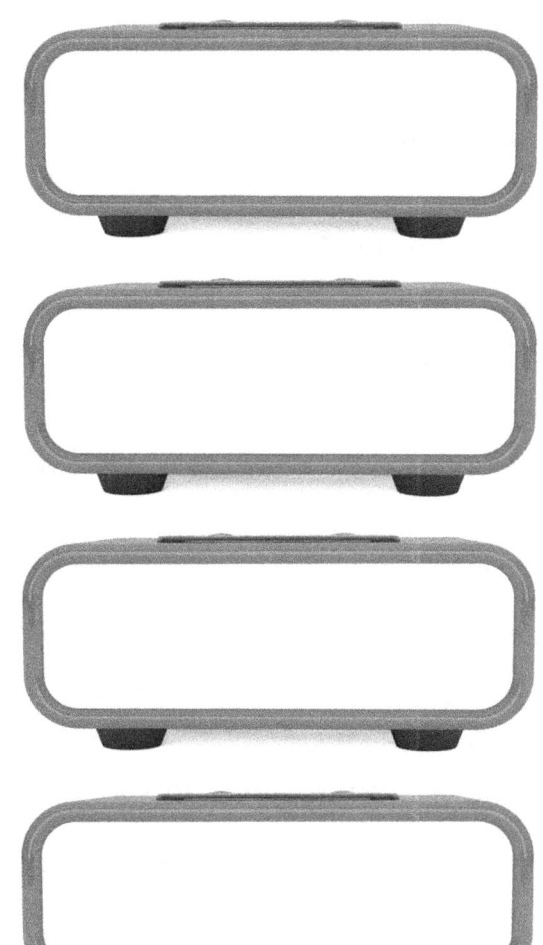

_____

_____

_____

Directions: Write times in the blanks to finish the story.

This morning, I woke up early. I was up at _____! I ate breakfast and finished by _____. I decided to watch a TV show that starts at _____. I lost track of time and realized I was running late to see my friend. I left the house at _____. I arrived at the park at _____, so I wasn't very late. We stayed at the park until _____. I was hungry, so I went home and ate lunch. I finished lunch at _____. I read a book until it was time to make dinner. Cooking took a long time. My mom and I cooked from _____ to _____. After we ate, I was tired. I went to bed at _____.

Name: _____ **Date:** _____

Directions: Trace each letter. Write your own letters to fill each line. Then, trace the sentence, and write it on your own.

i

I

j

J

o

O

I love orange jelly beans.

Name: _____ Date: _____

Directions: Trace each curved line and letter. Then, copy each row.

Name: _____ Date: _____

WEEK 22 DAY 2

Directions: Trace each letter. Then, practice writing your own letters.

Directions: Trace each letter. Then, copy the patterns.

Cursive Uppercase & Lowercase

© Shell Education 130196—180 Days of Cursive: Advanced

WEEK 22 DAY 3

Name: _____ Date: _____

Directions: Copy the words. Then, fill the lines.

will _____

whale _____

weigh _____

Directions: Use the words above to finish the sentences.

How much does a _____ _____ ? They look so big!

I saw one when I was at the beach.

I _____ get a book from the library to learn more.

Name: _____ Date: _____

WEEK 22 DAY 4

Directions: Solve each puzzle. What are the words and pictures saying?

_____ *rfa* _____   _____ *k* _____

som w r   _ri_
_v r_   _r un_
r inb w   _w r_

WEEK 22 DAY 5

Name: _____ **Date:** _____

Directions: Unscramble the letters. Then, write the words in cursive.

Clue: questions

hWat cloro si ti? _____
W__ a____ __r is it?

reehW ddi yeth og? _____
___r __i ___y ___?

hyW era yeth eerh? _____
___y ___r ___y ___r ?

ohW idd ouy llca? _____
___o __i __y u ___?

Wneh soed eht ovmie ttars? _____
___ n ___ s ___ m vi ___ s __r ?

wHo swa ryou prit? _____
___ s y ur __ri ?

Name: _____ Date: _____

WEEK 23
DAY 1

Directions: Trace each curved line and letter. Then, copy each row.

Directionality and Strokes

WEEK 23 DAY 2

Name: _____ Date: _____

Directions: Trace each letter. Then, practice writing your own letters.

Cursive Uppercase & Lowercase

Directions: Trace each letter. Then, copy the patterns.

Name: _____ Date: _____

Directions: Copy the name and words. Then, fill the lines.

Bodhi _____

bug _____

bought _____

Directions: Use the words above to finish the sentences.

Where did _____ go shopping?

He _____ a big glass box.

I wonder if he will put an animal in it like a _____ or a snake.

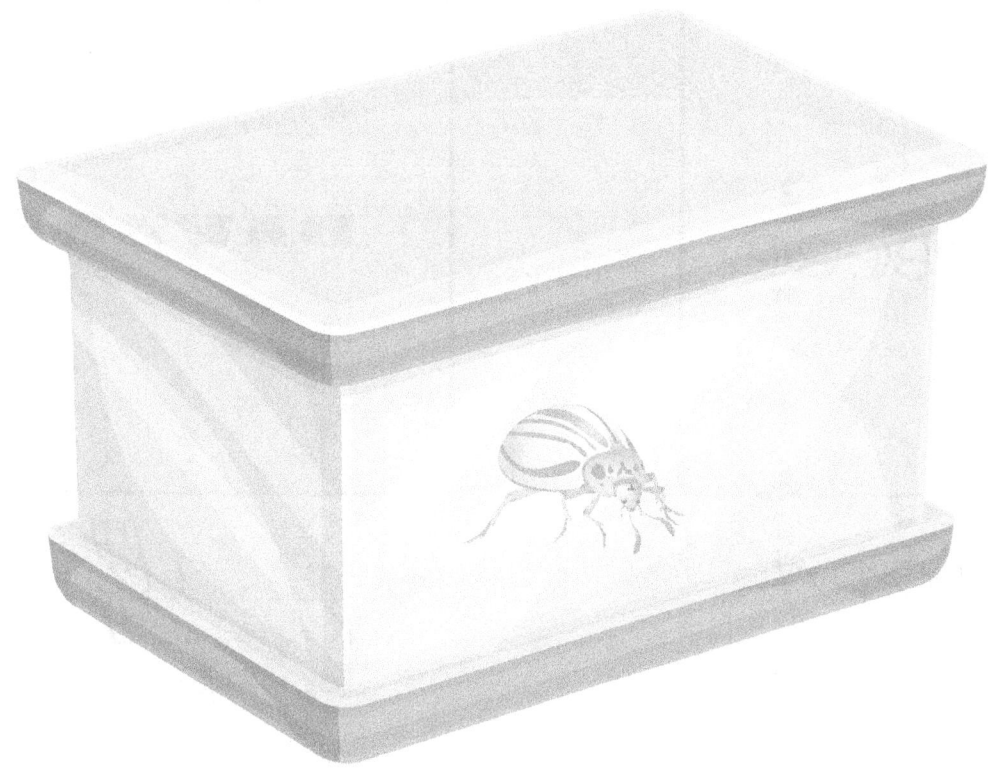

WEEK 23 DAY 4

Name: _____ Date: _____

Directions: Solve each puzzle. What are the words and pictures saying?

Think ▩

hink
_u si_
___ _x_

BILL1ON

_on in_
_i i n_

Beeeeee

long

BAKED

alf
_k_

Directions: Find rhyming words that match each definition.

tiny buzzing insect   _wee_____

naughty boy   _bad_____

dull taxi   _drab_____

crooked penny   _bent_____

superior bird home   _____

WEEK 24
DAY 1

Name: _____ Date: _____

Directions: Write the remaining dates in the calendar.

Directionality and Strokes

September

Sunday	Monday	Tuesday	Wednesday	Thursday	Friday	Saturday
			1	2		
	Labor Day					
Gio's birthday						
						baseball game
				30		

128   130196—180 Days of Cursive: Advanced   © Shell Education

Name: _____ **Date:** _____

WEEK 24
DAY 2

Directions: Trace each date. Then, practice writing your own dates.

1/23/2022

1/6/2020

3/26/1990

5/13/2020

6/12/21

7/30/2003

8/13/2022

9/30/2008

10/31/2023

12/25/2022

Numbers

WEEK 24 DAY 3

Name: _____ Date: _____

Directions: Trace the words. Use your best cursive to complete the prompts. Then, fill out the calendar.

My favorite month of
the year is _____
This month has ____ days.

Sentence Practice

| _____ |
| (name of month) |

130 130196—180 Days of Cursive: Advanced © Shell Education

Name: _____ **Date:** _____

WEEK 24 DAY 4

Directions: Complete the calendar for the month of your birthday. Draw a star on your birthday.

_____

Sunday	Monday	Tuesday	Wednesday	Thursday	Friday	Saturday

WEEK 24 DAY 5

Name: _____ Date: _____

Directions: Trace each letter. Then, write your own letters to fill each line.

Review

o _____

O _____

w _____

W _____

b _____

B _____

Name: _____ Date: _____

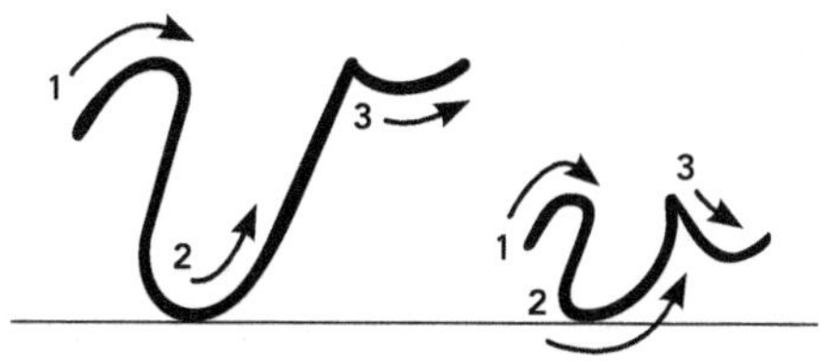

WEEK 25 DAY 1

Directions: Trace each curved line and letter. Then, copy each row.

Directionality and Strokes

WEEK 25 DAY 2

Name: _____ Date: _____

Directions: Trace each letter. Then, practice writing your own letters.

Directions: Trace each letter. Then, copy the patterns.

Name: _____ **Date:** _____

WEEK 25 DAY 3

Directions: Trace each sentence. Then, copy the sentences.

I have a beautiful cat.

I gave the dog a bath.

Give the cow hay.

Val ate a lot of food.

Sentence Practice

WEEK 25 DAY 4

Name: _____ **Date:** _____

Directions: Unscramble the letters. Then, write the words in cursive.

Clue: music

ioinlvn

oivce

esrrevs

ivel icsum

m s

bvratoi

ioalv

Name: _____ Date: _____

Directions: Fill in the missing letters to solve each riddle. Then, write a riddle for a friend to solve.

I'm a moving picture you can watch. What am I?

___ vid __

I'm someone who chooses to donate my time. What am I?

___ ___ n ___ r

I'm a break you take from work or school to relax. What am I?

___ acat __ n

_____

_____

_____

WEEK 26
DAY 1

Name: _____ Date: _____

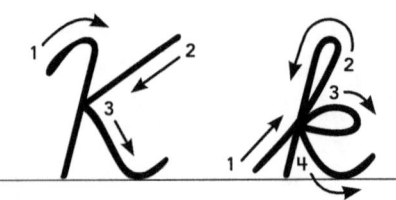

Directions: Trace each curved line and letter. Then, copy each row.

(handwriting practice rows for cursive l, e, k, j, and K)

Name: _____ Date: _____

WEEK 26 DAY 2

Directions: Trace each letter. Then, practice writing your own letters.

k k k k k k k k k k k k

k

k

K K K K K K K K K K

K

K

Directions: Trace each letter. Then, copy the patterns.

KKkk kkkk KKkk kkkk KKkk

KKkk kkkk KKkk kkkk KKkk

Cursive Uppercase & Lowercase

WEEK 26 DAY 3

Name: _____ Date: _____

Directions: Trace each sentence. Then, copy the sentences.

Sentence Practice

Kayla will go to Italy.

I packed a bag for the trip.

We will keep the luggage at the hotel.

The van will pick it up.

Name: _____ Date: _____

Directions: Find rhyming words that match each definition.

dark colored sled dog   *dusky*

light red beverage   *pink*

smelly animal's bed   *skunk*

false reptile   *fake*

bag carried on your shoulders _____

WEEK 26 DAY 5

Name: _____ Date: _____

Directions: Use your best cursive to answer the questions.

What is your favorite color?

_____

What is your favorite sport?

_____

How many sisters do you have?

_____

How many brothers do you have?

_____

When did you wake up?

_____

Where do you want to visit?

_____

Review

Name: _____ Date: _____

WEEK 27 DAY 1

Directions: Write your address in the top left corner of the envelope.

Felipe Estrada
321 Center Street
Old Town, TX 12345

Directionality and Strokes

WEEK 27 DAY 2

Name: _____ Date: _____

Directions: Trace each zip code. Then, practice writing your own zip code. Note that zip codes do not need commas.

Numbers

55555 _____

90210 _____

32707 _____

69543 _____

46783 _____

52826 _____

67890 _____

72341 _____

86543 _____

92345 _____

Directions: Read the envelope. Then, use your best cursive to answer the questions.

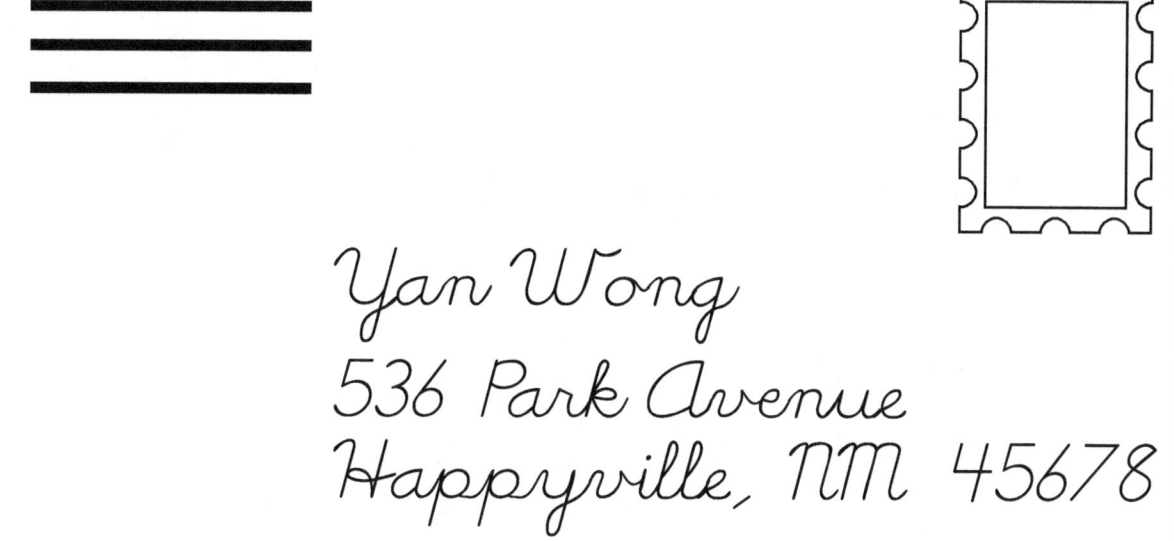

Who is this letter addressed to?

_____

What is the street address?

_____

What is the zip code?

_____

WEEK 27 DAY 4

Name: _____ Date: _____

Directions: Write a friendly letter to go inside this envelope.

Activity

John Smith
123 Main Street
Grandville, FL 55555

Zara Grant
606 High Street
Happyville, NM 55555

_____,

_____

_____

_____

_____

_____,

_____

Name: _____ **Date:** _____

WEEK 27
DAY 5

Directions: Trace each letter. Write your own letters to fill each line. Then, trace the sentence, and write it on your own.

b

B

v

V

k

K

Books are in the very back.

Review

WEEK 28 DAY 1

Name: _____ **Date:** _____

Directions: Trace each curved line and letter. Then, copy each row.

Name: _____ Date: _____

WEEK 28
DAY 2

Directions: Trace each letter. Then, practice writing your own letters.

n n n n n n n n n n n n

n

n

R R R R R R R R R R R R

R

R

Directions: Trace each letter. Then, copy the patterns.

Rn Rn Rn Rn Rn Rn Rn Rn

Rnn Rnn Rnn Rnn Rnn Rnn Rnn

nnnRnnnRnnnRnnnRnnn

Cursive Uppercase & Lowercase

WEEK 28 DAY 3

Name: _____ **Date:** _____

Directions: Trace each sentence. Then, copy the sentences.

I like to read.

Rhea got a book at the library.

We read together at the library.

Are you at the library, too?

Directions: Find rhyming words that match the definition.

fright caused by a grizzly   _bear_

intelligent beginning   _smart_

tall stack of roses   _flower_

odd facial hair   _weird_

insect carpet   _____

WEEK 28 DAY 5

Name: _____ Date: _____

Directions: Use your best cursive to answer the questions.

What color is your shirt?

_____

Who is your teacher?

_____

When will you eat dinner?

_____

Where do you keep your socks?

_____

How many hats do you have?

_____

Review

Name: _____ **Date:** _____

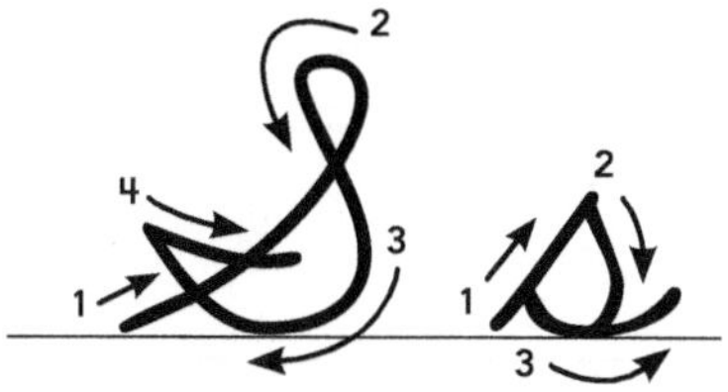

WEEK 29 DAY 1

Directions: Trace each curved line and letter. Then, copy each row.

Directionality and Strokes

WEEK 29 DAY 2

Name: _____ Date: _____

Directions: Trace each letter. Then, practice writing your own letters.

Directions: Trace each letter. Then, copy the patterns.

Cursive Uppercase & Lowercase

154 130196—180 Days of Cursive: Advanced © Shell Education

Name: _____ Date: _____

Directions: Trace each sentence. Then, copy the sentences.

Is purple a pretty color?

She likes that color.

I see a purple flower outside.

The flowers are pretty.

WEEK 29 DAY 4

Name: _____ **Date:** _____

Directions: Solve each puzzle. What are the words and pictures saying?

Activity

READ
_____ between the lines

be_____n
th_____n

PROMISE (broken)
br_____n
_____om

EGGS over EASY
_____ over
_____ y

NO/SE (no through se)
_____ ken
n_____

Name: _____ Date: _____

Directions: Use your best cursive to answer the questions. Use full sentences.

What is your hobby?

_____

_____

What is your favorite part of your hobby?

_____

_____

Why do you like to do your hobby?

_____

_____

How did you learn about your hobby?

_____

_____

Directions: Color the numbers.

Name: _____ Date: _____

Directions: Trace each amount. Then, practice writing your own amounts. Remember to add a dollar sign before the amount.

$3.50

$1.00

$15.35

$3.17

$40.50

$500.00

$6.15

$7000.00

$42.73

$10.32

$4.56 + $3.24 =

$16.00 − $4.72 =

$12.05 + $7.95 =

WEEK 30 DAY 3

Name: _____ Date: _____

Directions: Use complete sentences to answer the questions in your best cursive.

$3.50 $16.75 $3.25 $12.50

How much is the kite?

_____

How much are the bananas?

_____

How much is the car?

_____

How much is the sweater?

_____

Name: _____   Date: _____

WEEK 30 DAY 4

Directions: Write your own prices to complete the story.

   I went to the store to shop for a party. I bought decorations first. Balloons cost _____, streamers cost _____, and a banner cost _____. It was not very expensive. Next, I went to the grocery store to buy food. Drinks cost _____, chips cost _____, and crackers cost _____. I wanted more healthy snacks, so I bought some fruit for _____ and vegetables for _____. The last thing I bought was pizza. It cost _____.

WEEK 30 DAY 5

Name: _____ **Date:** _____

Directions: Trace each letter. Write your own letters to fill each line. Then, trace the sentence, and write it on your own.

k _____

K _____

r _____

R _____

s _____

S _____

Red kites fill the summer sky. _____

Review

Name: _____ Date: _____

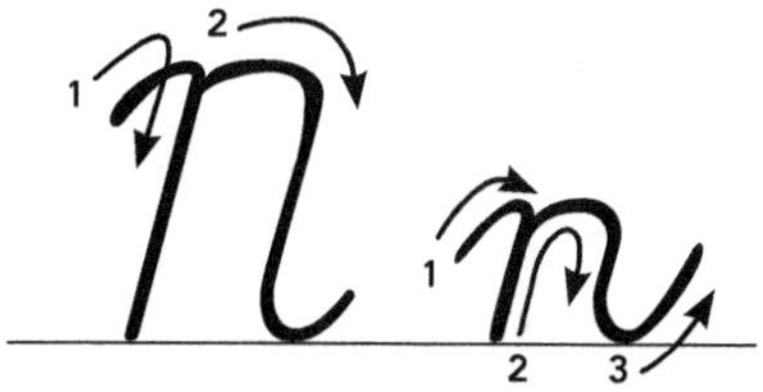

WEEK 31 DAY 1

Directions: Trace each curved line and letter. Then, copy each row.

Directionality and Strokes

WEEK 31 DAY 2

Name: _____ Date: _____

Directions: Trace each letter. Then, practice writing your own letters.

Directions: Trace each letter. Then, copy the patterns.

Name: _____ **Date:** _____

WEEK 31 DAY 3

Directions: Trace each sentence. Then, copy the sentences.

I can read the clock.

When can we go home?

Nia is ready to leave.

I think we should go.

Sentence Practice

WEEK 31 DAY 4

Name: _____ Date: _____

Directions: Unscramble the letters. Then, write the words in cursive.

Clue: numbers

eno

_____

ent hsandout

_____

eevsn

_____

levene

_____

innety-nnie

_____

eno unhdred

_____

Name: _____ Date: _____

Directions: Use your best cursive to answer the questions. Use full sentences.

Where is your favorite place to be? Why?

_____

_____

_____

What is your favorite holiday? Why?

_____

_____

_____

What was the last thing you learned? Describe it.

_____

_____

_____

WEEK 32 DAY 1

Name: _____ Date: _____

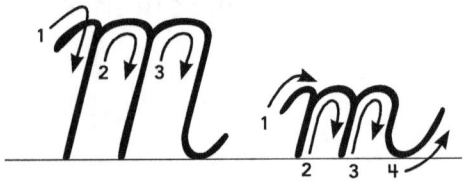

Directionality and Strokes

Directions: Trace each curved line and letter. Then, copy each row.

Name: _____ Date: _____

Directions: Trace each letter. Then, practice writing your own letters.

m m m m m m m m m m

m

m

M M M M M M M M M

M

M

Directions: Trace each letter. Then, copy the patterns.

Mm Mm Mm Mm Mm

Mm Mm Mm Mm Mm

mM mM mM mM mM

WEEK 32 DAY 3

Name: _____ Date: _____

Directions: Trace each sentence. Then, copy the sentences.

Mia likes to watch movies.

What movies do you like?

Funny movies are my favorite.

Funny movies are called comedies.

Sentence Practice

WEEK 32 DAY 4

Name: _____ Date: _____

Directions: Solve the riddles. Use your best cursive to write the answers. Then, write your own riddle for someone to solve.

Where are the lakes always empty, the mountains always flat, and the rivers always still?

_____ ____*ap*____

If you drop me, I'm sure to crack, but smile at me, and I'll always smile back. What am I?

_____ _____*ror*____

What belongs to you, but your friends use it more than you?

__*yo*____ ____*na*____

_____

_____

_____

Activity

WEEK 32 DAY 5

Name: _____ Date: _____

Directions: Write a letter to a friend about a game or sport you like. Write what you like about it. Remember to sign your name at the end.

Name: _____

Street Address: _____

City: _____ State: _____ Zip code: _____

Dear _____,

_____

_____

_____

_____

_____

_____

                                                                                         _____

                                                                                         _____

Review

Name: _____ Date: _____

WEEK 33 DAY 1

Directions: Trace the numbers. Then, color the picture.

(555) 690-7577

(555) 690-7577

Directions: Write a phone number you know. Then, color the picture.

Directionality and Strokes

© Shell Education 130196—180 Days of Cursive: Advanced 173

WEEK 33 DAY 2

Name: _____ Date: _____

Directions: Trace each number. Then, practice writing your own numbers.

(813)555-3209

(654)555-2345

(454)555-7863

(905)555-7245

(626)555-9824

(690)555-9021

(321)555-7823

Numbers

Name: _____ Date: _____

WEEK 33 DAY 3

Directions: Read the phone numbers. Then, answer the questions.

Contacts

Yaal
(123) 555-6734

Sharon
(813) 555-6279

Kevin
(407) 734-6435

Chris
(543) 372-9387

What is Sharon's phone number?

_____

What is Yaal's phone number?

_____

What is Chris's phone number?

_____

What is Kevin's phone number?

_____

WEEK 33 DAY 4

Name: _____ **Date:** _____

Directions: Write a letter to a friend to share your contact information. Include your address and your phone number in the letter.

_____

_____

_____

Dear _____,

Name: _____ Date: _____

WEEK 33
DAY 5

Directions: Trace each letter. Write your own letters to fill each line. Then, trace the sentence, and write it on your own.

S _____

s _____

N _____

n _____

M _____

m _____

Mr. Samuels is nice. _____

Review

Name: _____ Date: _____

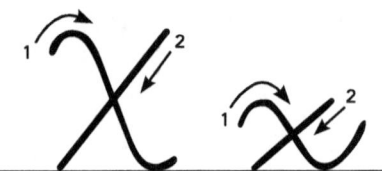

Directionality and Strokes

Directions: Trace each curved line and letter. Then, copy each row.

Name: _____ Date: _____

WEEK 34 DAY 2

Directions: Trace each letter. Then, practice writing your own letters.

Directions: Trace each letter. Then, copy the patterns.

Cursive Uppercase & Lowercase

WEEK 34 DAY 3

Name: _____   Date: _____

Directions: Trace each sentence. Then, copy the sentences.

Xavier broke his arm.

He got an x-ray.

I texted him to ask how he felt.

Max checked on him, too.

Xavier said he is feeling better now.

Name: _____ **Date:** _____

Directions: Use your best cursive to answer each question in complete sentences.

Where do you want to travel?

_____

_____

Why do you want to travel there?

_____

_____

How do you get there?

_____

_____

Who do you want to travel with?

_____

_____

What will you do there?

_____

_____

WEEK 34 DAY 5

Name: _____ Date: _____

Directions: Write a letter to a friend about your favorite book. Write about your favorite characters and what you like about it. Remember to sign your name at the end.

Name: _____

Street Address: _____

City: _____ State: _____ Zip code: _____

Dear _____,

_____

_____

_____

_____

_____

_____

_____

                                                  _____

                                                  _____

Review

Name: _____ **Date:** _____

Directions: Trace each curved line and letter. Then, copy each row.

WEEK 35 DAY 2

Name: _____ Date: _____

Directions: Trace each letter. Then, practice writing your own letters.

Directions: Trace each letter. Then, copy the patterns.

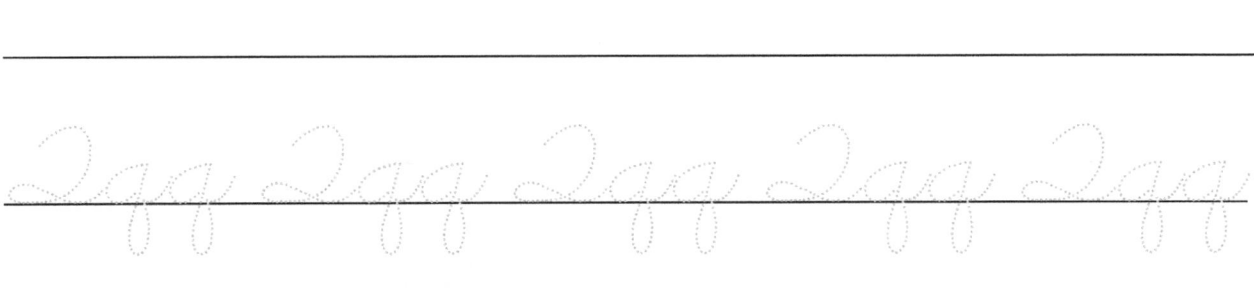

Name: _____ Date: _____

Directions: Copy the words. Then, fill the lines.

quickly
_____

quiet
_____

question
_____

Directions: Use the words above to finish the sentences.

May I ask a _____ ?

_____ jumped out of the way.

I was very _____ when my sister took a nap.

WEEK 35 DAY 4

Name: _____ Date: _____

Directions: Find rhyming words that match each definition.

fast baby chicken   *quick* _____

unkind king's wife   *mean* _____

respond with duck sounds   *quack* _____

pretend earthquake   *fake* _____

good test taker   _____

Name: _____ Date: _____

Directions: Write a journal entry about your favorite vacation. Write the date at the top of the entry.

Date: _____

WEEK 36 DAY 1

Name: _____ Date: _____

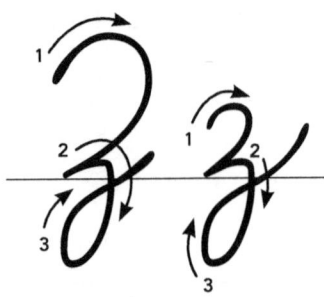

Directions: Trace each curved line and letter. Then, copy each row.

Name: _____ Date: _____

WEEK 36 DAY 2

Directions: Trace each letter. Then, practice writing your own letters.

Cursive Uppercase & Lowercase

Directions: Trace each letter. Then, copy the patterns.

WEEK 36 DAY 3

Name: _____ Date: _____

Directions: Trace each sentence. Then, copy the sentences.

Zach likes animals.

_____

His favorite animal is a zebra.

_____

Zara likes music.

_____

Jazz is her favorite.

_____

Name: _____ Date: _____

WEEK 36 DAY 4

Directions: Trace the words. Practice writing the sentence two times on your own.

The quick brown fox jumps over the lazy dog.

WEEK 36 DAY 5

Name: _____ Date: _____

Directions: Write a review of your favorite movie. Why did you like it?

Title: _____

Review

Lowercase Letter Guide

Appendix

 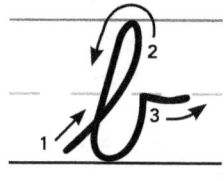 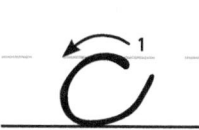 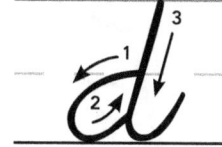 
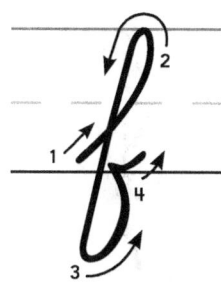  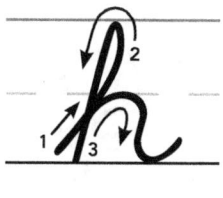 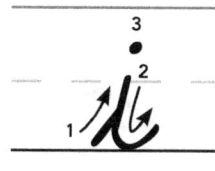 
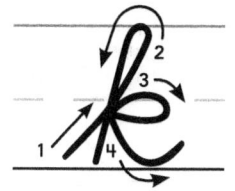   
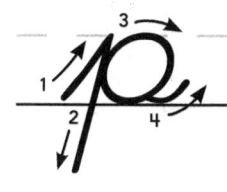 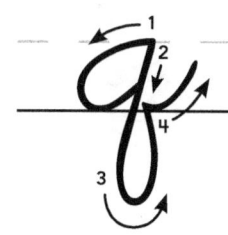 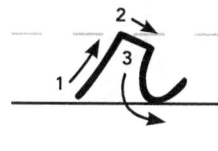 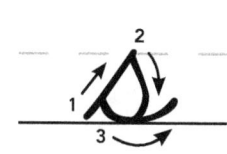 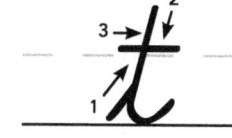

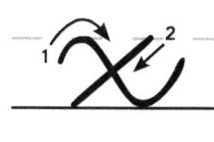 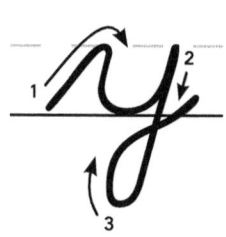 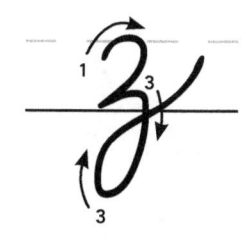

Appendix
Uppercase Letter Guide

  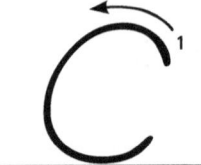  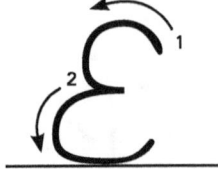

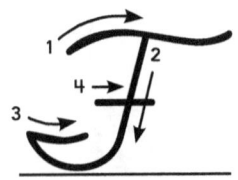 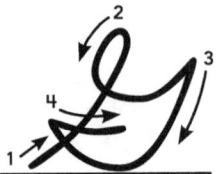 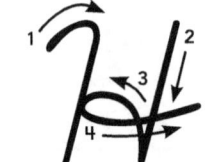 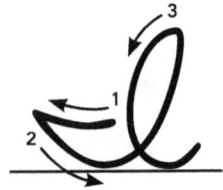 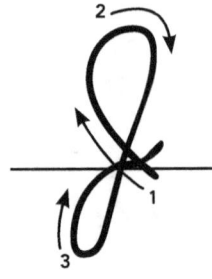

 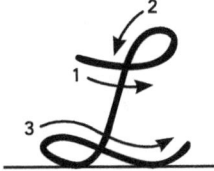  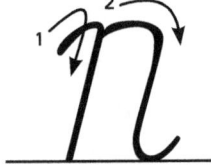 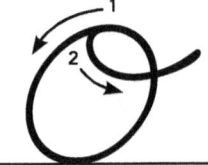

 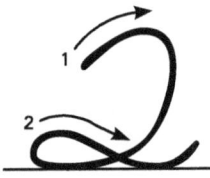 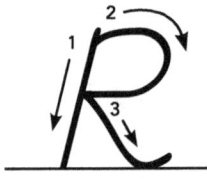 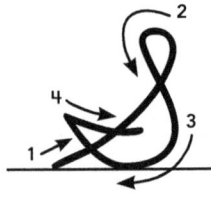 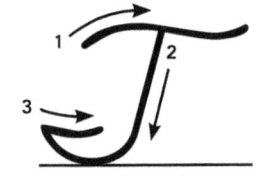

 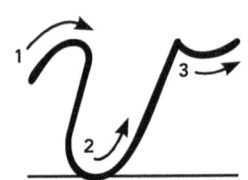 

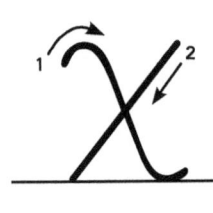 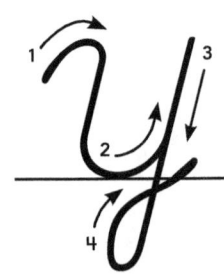 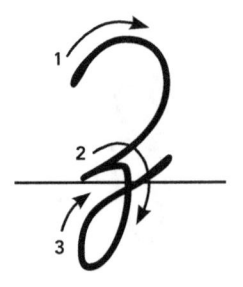

Number Guide

Appendix

1 2 3 4 5

6 7 8 9 0

Appendix

Answer Key

There are many open-ended pages and writing prompts in this book. For those activities, the answers will vary. Examples are given as needed.

Week 1 Day 4 (page 16)

Week 1 Day 5 (page 17)

zucchini
cucumber
celery
carrot
lettuce
broccoli

Week 2 Day 4 (page 21)

an ape
an alligator
an armadillo

Week 2 Day 5 (page 22)

alligator
jaguar
camel
ape
armadillo
cheetah

Week 3 Day 4 (page 26)

downtown
download
3D movie
eye shadow

Week 3 Day 5 (page 27)

a desert
the dictionary
a cold

Week 5 Day 4 (page 36)

vegetables
good afternoon
forget it
way to go

Week 5 Day 5 (page 37)

green
orange
bright yellow
gray
beige
magenta

Week 6 Day 4 (page 41)

lemonade
tea bag
breakfast
forehead

Week 6 Day 5 (page 42)

the letter E
seven
age

Week 7 Day 4 (page 46)

climb a mountain
go hang gliding
learn to drive
listen to music
land an airplane
fly a kite

Answer Key (cont.) — Appendix

Week 7 Day 5 (page 47)

a towel   gloves
light

Week 9 Day 4 (page 56)

forty years   foreign film
waterfall   comfortable

Week 9 Day 5 (page 57)

thankful   hopeful
fierce   frustrated
joyful   flustered

Week 10 Day 4 (page 61)

touchdown   highway
honeybee   tunafish

Week 10 Day 5 (page 62)

a hole
they're shellfish.
a mushroom

Week 11 Day 4 (page 66)

thunder
a teapot
trouble

Week 11 Day 5 (page 67)

palm tree   violet
tulip   cactus
mint   water lily

Week 13 Day 4 (page 76)

apple pie   up to you
wake up   potato

Week 13 Day 5 (page 77)

apple   grape
papaya   pineapple
apricot   plum

Week 14 Day 4 (page 81)

try to   once upon
understand   a time
misunderstood   swim underwater

Week 14 Day 5 (page 82)

number slumber
pie guy
butter cutter
funny bunny
mouse house

Week 15 Day 2 (page 84)

13,000   7,000
5,000

Week 15 Day 4 (page 86)

2	3	4	1
4	1	3	2
1	4	2	3
3	2	1	4

4	1	2	3
3	2	4	1
1	4	3	2
2	3	1	4

3	4	1	2
1	2	3	4
4	3	2	1
2	1	4	3

Appendix

Answer Key (cont.)

Week 16 Day 4 (page 91)

many thanks   look me in the eye
way to go   history repeats itself

Week 16 Day 5 (page 92)

happily   mysteriously
sadly   beautifully
angrily   carefully

Week 17 Day 4 (page 96)

foreign language   missing you
fishing hook   one in a million

Week 17 Day 5 (page 97)

fish dish   thick stick
fine pine   rabbit habit
pig wig

Week 19 Day 4 (page 106)

jump   jog
juggle   journal
joke   jiggle

Week 19 Day 5 (page 107)

jelly
juice
a jewel

Week 21 Day 1 (page 113)

broken heart   top secret
big bad wolf   book ends

Week 20 Day 4 (page 112)

loud crowd
frog jog
book crook
top cop
hot tot

Week 22 Day 4 (page 121)

waterfall   wake up
somewhere over the rainbow   trip around the world

Week 22 Day 5 (page 122)

What color is it?
Where did they go?
Why are they here?
Who did you call?
When does the movie start?
How was your trip?

Week 23 Day 4 (page 126)

think outside the box   one in a billion
belong   half baked

Answer Key (cont.)

Week 23 Day 5 (page 127)

wee bee
bad lad
drab cab
bent cent
best nest

Week 25 Day 4 (page 136)

violin
voice
verse
live music
vibrato
viola

Week 25 Day 5 (page 137)

a video
a volunteer
a vacation

Week 26 Day 4 (page 141)

dusky husky
pink drink
skunk bunk
fake snake
backpack

Week 28 Day 4 (page 151)

bear scare
smart start
flower tower
bug rug
weird beard

Week 29 Day 4 (page 156)

read between the lines
eggs over easy
broken promise
broken nose

Week 30 Day 2 (page 159)

$17.80
$11.28
$20.00

Week 31 Day 4 (page 166)

one
ten thousand
seven
eleven
ninety-one
one hundred

Week 32 Day 4 (page 171)

a map
a mirror
your name

Week 35 Day 4 (page 186)

quick chick
mean queen
quack back
quiz wiz
fake quake

Appendix

Suggested Websites

Website Title	Address	Content
ABC Mouse	www.abcmouse.com	alphabet, phonics
Learning A–Z	www.learninga-z.com	alphabet, phonics
Student Handouts	www.studenthandouts.com	alphabet

Digital Resources

Accessing the Digital Resources

The digital resources can be downloaded by following these steps:

1. Go to **www.tcmpub.com/digital**
2. Use the ISBN number to redeem the digital resources.
3. Respond to the question using the book.
4. Follow the prompts on the Content Cloud website to sign in or create a new account.
5. The redeemed content will now be on your My Content screen. Click on the product to look through the Digital Resources. All files can be downloaded, while some files can also be previewed, opened, and shared.
    - Please note: Some files provided for download have large file sizes. Download times for these larger files vary based on your download speed.

Contents of the Digital Resources

Activities

- Hands-on practice for writing uppercase and lowercase letters
- Sentence-writing practice
- Handwriting lines for cursive activities

www.ingramcontent.com/pod-product-compliance
Lightning Source LLC
Chambersburg PA
CBHW060421010526
44118CB00017B/2305